SWEET POTATO STORIES

SIX STORIES ON PROBLEM SOLVING
FOR STUDENTS IN PRESCHOOL-3RD GRADES

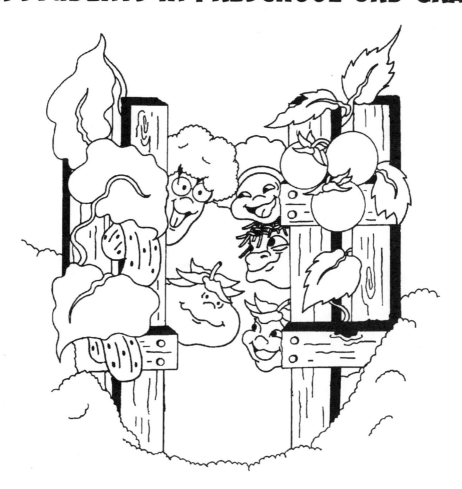

by
Kay Farmer & Cindy Yarberry

Illustrated by
Cameon Smith-Funk

Revised/Reprinted 1998
Copyright © 1990
mar★co products, inc.

Published by
mar★co products, inc.
1443 Old York Road
Warminster, PA 18974
1-800-448-2197

Library of Congress Catalog Card Number: 98-84909

ISBN: 1-57543-013-4

Printed in the U.S.A.

CONTENTS

INTRODUCTION

Sweet Potato Stories can be used with individual students or in a large- or small-group setting. Each story can be used for a one-session lesson or all six stories can be used for a six-session group on problem solving. Through the use of interesting stories, finger puppets and creative thinking, the *Sweet Potato Stories* present ways for educators to implement creative problem-solving techniques. Each story deals with a common childhood situation and includes discussion questions, follow-up activities, and reproducible activity pages. Also included with the book are finger puppets representing the characters in the stories.

FINGER PUPPETS:
Puppets are an excellent way to enhance a story. Introduce the appropriate finger puppets to your students before reading the story. If you are not comfortable using puppets, you may want to practice in front of the mirror before presenting the puppets to the students. The puppets are also used in some follow-up role-playing activities. When participating in this type of activity, students often identify with the puppets, and become comfortable enough to share their personal experiences with the group.

PROBLEM-SOLVING:
Suggestions for solving problems creatively are listed on the following page and identified when they appear in a story. You may wish to address these techniques as you read the story or go back to them during the follow-up discussion. Before beginning each story, discuss the problem-solving steps with the students. Doing this will help the students identify the problem in the story and think of ways to resolve it.

QUESTIONS FOR DISCUSSION:
Questions included at the end of each story may be presented to the students for oral answers. The students' responses will help you determine how well they understood the story.

FOLLOW-UP ACTIVITIES:
Follow-up activities are found at the end of each story. Choose any or all of the activities that will help the students understand the concept and how to deal with the situation each story describes.

SOLVING PROBLEMS CREATIVELY

IDENTIFY THE PROBLEM:

Be sure students can correctly identify the problem. For example: The true problem may be lying; the result may be not having any friends.

LIST THE ALTERNATIVES:

Have the students suggest alternatives before reading those listed in the story. The alternatives in the story are only suggestions, and should not be regarded as the only possible solutions. Accept all alternatives the students suggest as these ideas are forms of self-expression.

CHOOSE AN ALTERNATIVE:

After reading the alternatives listed in the story, discuss them and those the students have suggested. Be sure to mention a possible result of each alternative. Allow the students to choose the alternative they would try first. Do not try to influence students' choices, but lead a discussion on the consequences of the alternatives suggested.

IMPLEMENT A CHOICE:

If necessary, encourage the students to role-play each of the alternatives chosen. This will help give them self-confidence when implementing these alternatives with their peers.

SWEET POTATO

Making Friends

"Hi! My name is Sweet Potato. I live here in the *Good Neighbor Garden.* It sure is nice to see the veggies playing so well together, but it hasn't always been this way. I can remember in the spring when the veggies were just sprouts. We seemed to have a problem every day. They just could not get along with each other."

"I want you to meet all the veggies in the *Good Neighbor Garden,*" continued Sweet Potato. "They know that making new friends can be difficult, and they may have some ideas to share with you."

IDENTIFY THE PROBLEM

"Hi! My name is Ben Broccoli. Sometimes the other veggies call me *Brains.* I don't like that nickname, but I do like to study and learn. I'm tall and green with lots of bushy hair."

"My name is Tim Tomato. I feel shy lots of the time. I'm red and round. I like to play ball and have fun with everybody."

"Hello. My name is Sally Strawberry. I'm red, too. I have lots of brothers and sisters in the berry patch. I like to jump rope and play with everybody's toys."

"And, I'm Lucy Lettuce. I'm green and I have lots of curly hair. My favorite thing to do is play with my hula hoop. I'm pretty good at twirling it around."

"Do you remember when you were all just sprouts trying to become friends?" asked Sweet Potato.

"I sure do," answered Tim. "It was really hard for me, because I was so shy!"

"I remember when people called me names," Sally Strawberry chimed in. "I didn't have any friends."

"I'm glad you remember," replied Sweet Potato. "Let's make a list of some of the things that helped you feel more comfortable about making new friends."

#1
#2
#3
#4
#5

LIST YOUR ALTERNATIVES

"One thing to remember," said Ben Broccoli, "is that it's OK to have a friend who's different than you. Your friend may be a different color from you. You may not be the same size or age, or you may not talk in the same way."

"That's right, Ben," replied Sweet Potato. "We may be different in some ways, but alike in other ways. We all have feelings. We *all* need friends."

"Another thing to remember," added Lucy Lettuce, "is that it is important to be forgiving, understanding, and loyal if you want to have good friends."

"You're right, Lucy," Sweet Potato answered. "If you try to put yourself in the other person's place, you will find it easier to understand him or her. Understanding people makes it easier to forgive them and stand by them."

"I think it is important to remember that you can have more than one friend at a time," added Sally Strawberry.

"I agree with you, Sally," answered Sweet Potato. "When I think of all the fun I've had being friends with all of you, I would be sad if only one of you could be my friend."

16

"I learned that making friends doesn't have to be hard," said Tim Tomato. "If you just smile and act friendly, people will usually smile and be friendly right back to you!"

"I'm proud of all of you for sharing what you have learned about making friends," Sweet Potato said with a smile. "Maybe the boys and girls who have been listening to your ideas would like to try one of them. Or maybe they have some ideas of their own they would like to share."

CHOOSE AN ALTERNATIVE

"I wonder which idea you will choose to use the next time *you* want to make friends?" asked Sweet Potato.

IMPLEMENT YOUR CHOICE

QUESTIONS FOR DISCUSSION

1. What is a *friend?*
   (Allow the students to share their ideas about the meaning of being a friend. Accept any answer.)

2. What do you like most about your friends?
   (Make a list of the qualities the students name and, if desired, write them on the chalkboard or a large piece of paper. Introduce words like loyal, understanding, and forgiving and explain the meaning of each word to the group.)

3. What are some characteristics that would *not* be found in a good friend?
   (Accept any answers and, if desired, write them on the chalkboard or on a large piece of paper.)

4. Name something about yourself that would make you a good friend to others.
   (Ask each student in the group to name one thing about him/herself. Be sure each student gives at least one answer.)

5. Is it OK to have more than one friend at a time? Why or why not?
   (Accept any answer, but make sure the students explain the reasons for their answers.)

6. Are all friends the same?
   (No. Point out that our best friends are usually a lot like us. They usually like the same kinds of things, may be about the same age, and usually live nearby. Point out that although there are similarities, there may also be differences in race, size, looks, handicapping conditions, etc.)

7. Do you know someone who needs a friend? Without naming him/her, what can you do to help?
   (If the student's answer is "yes," ask the second part of the question. Try to get each student to make a commitment to do something with the person identified as needing a friend.)

FOLLOW-UP ACTIVITIES

1. VISUALIZATION EXERCISE

Ask the students to close their eyes and think about someone they like. The person they think about may be anyone, another child or an adult. After a few minutes, tell the students to open their eyes. Ask each student to describe the person he/she thought about and how that person makes him/her feel.

2. THE NAME GAME

Write each student's name vertically on a sheet of paper before the lesson begins. Explain to the students that they are to provide a positive adjective, describing a friendly trait for each letter of their names. If it is necessary to give the students an example, select a name no one in the class has. For younger children, use only the first letter of the name. Display these examples throughout the room. Examples: (Kate) **K**ind, **A**greeable, **T**errific, **E**nergetic.

3. AUTOGRAPH BOOK

Fold several sheets of paper and staple them into book form for each student. Distribute these autograph books and ask the students to design their own covers and titles. Tell the students to keep their books with them throughout the day and collect signatures of other students.

4. WHAT WOULD YOU DO?

Give each student in the group a copy of page 21. Review the page with the students. Have them complete the page.

5. FIND A FRIEND

Give each student in the group a copy of page 22 and tell them to find others in the room who have the characteristics described on the page. When the student finds a friend with that characteristic, the student should ask the friend to sign his/her name on the line in the appropriate box. After the students have completed this game, discuss the similarities and differences they share with their friends.

WHAT WOULD YOU DO?

Circle the alternatives that you want to remember the next time you want to make a new friend.

| A friend can be different from me. | A good friend is understanding, forgiving, and loyal. |
| I can have more than one friend. | Smile and act friendly. |

DRAW A PICTURE OF YOU AND A FRIEND.

FIND A FRIEND

Name: _____

Shoes that tie	Eyes that are brown
_____	_____
Hair that is curly	Hands that are the same size as mine
_____	_____
Someone who is the same height as me	Someone who wears glasses
_____	_____

BEN BROCCOLI

Name-Calling

"Hello! I'm Sweet Potato, and I live here in the *Good Neighbor Garden*. Today I'll be visiting Miss Asparagus' class at the *Good Neighbor Garden School*. Why don't you come with me?"

GOOD
NEIGHBOR
GARDEN
SCHOOL

$$1+1=2$$
$$2+2=4$$
$$3+3=6$$

Some of the students in the class have been misbehaving. Miss Asparagus has been speaking to them.

"Ben," said Miss Asparagus, "you will have to stay after school today."

"Please put your pencils in your hand instead of sticking them in your nose! I just can't understand how you have been acting lately."

"Ben, you look like you need a friend," said Sweet Potato.

"I sure could use a friend, Sweet Potato," Ben exclaimed. "I feel awful and I'm confused. When I used to do my best at school, the kids teased me and called me *Brains Broccoli.* I don't like being different. I wanted the kids to like me, so I decided to change."

Test Today

"At first," Ben went on, "everyone thought I was cool. They laughed when I acted silly and when I made fun of the teacher. I felt like I was part of the gang."

"Bozo Broccoli! I wish the old 'Brains' was back!" whispered Sally.

"But I guess I was wrong," Ben admitted. "They're not laughing any more. The kids don't like me. The teacher doesn't like me. I don't even like myself!"

"Ben, it's OK to be yourself," said Sweet Potato. "You're a good student and you've worked hard at being your best. I hope you realize that no matter what you do, some people are going to call you names. Let's see if we can think of some things you can do when that happens."

"Thank you, Sweet Potato. I'll give that a try," replied Ben.

#1
#2
#3
#4
#5

LIST YOUR ALTERNATIVES

"I could move to another school," suggested Ben.

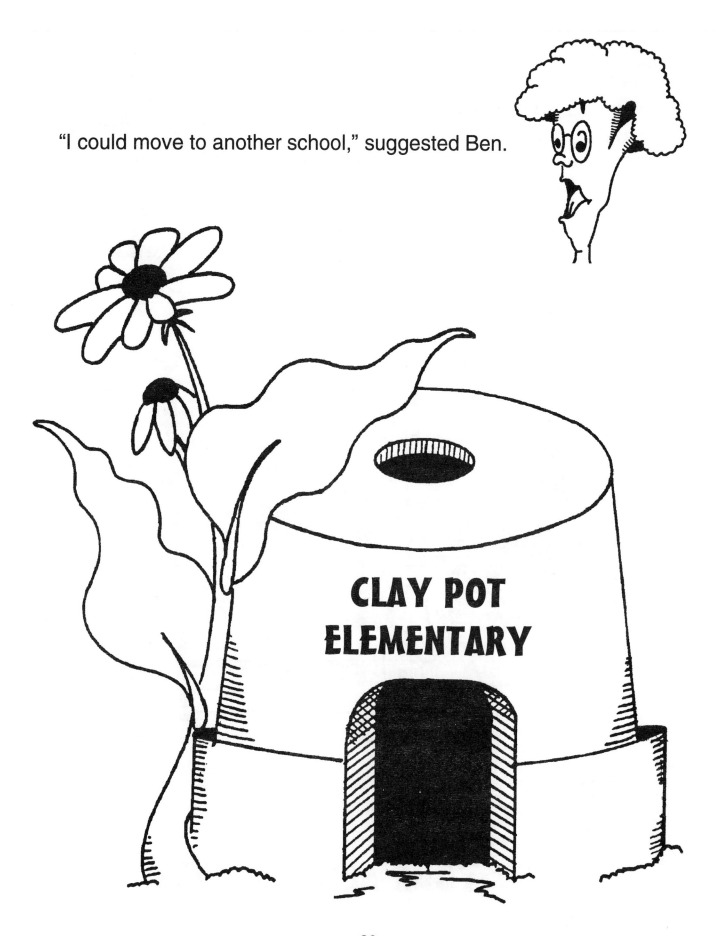

"I could just ignore the other kids," he added.

Please don't call me that. I don't like it.

"Or maybe I could tell them that I don't like it and nicely ask them to stop."

"I could call them names, too."

Freckle Face!
Freckle Face!

Ben continued, "Maybe, I should just accept 'Brains' as a name. It's really not that bad, and I know the other kids are still my friends."

"I like your list, Ben," said Sweet Potato. "Now, look at each of your choices and decide what you might do the next time someone calls you a name. If you try one thing and it doesn't seem to be working, don't give up. You may try something else or talk about it again."

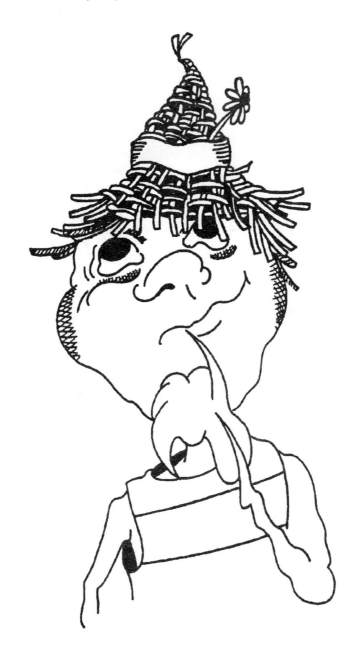

I wonder which choice Ben Broccoli will try? What would you do?

IMPLEMENT YOUR CHOICE

QUESTIONS FOR DISCUSSION

1. What was Ben confused about at the beginning of the story?
   (Ben did not know how to act in order to make the other children like him. They made fun of Ben because he was smart, so he thought they would like him better if he acted silly. But they didn't like that, either.)

2. Have you ever felt like you were different from the other kids?
   (Accept any answer.)

3. Have you ever disliked someone because he/she was different? After getting to know that person better, did that difference matter? Did you feel differently about him/her, then?
   (Accept any answers.)

4. List some ways your friends are different from you.
   (List the students' answers on the chalkboard or on a large piece of paper.)

5. Did Ben's friends intend to hurt his feelings when they called him "Brains"?
   (Probably not. Name-calling is not always intended to hurt feelings. Sometimes it is meant as a compliment.)

6. Did Ben's friends like it when Ben tried to change and acted like someone he really was not?
   (No.)

7. Was Ben happy with the change?
   (No.)

8. Have you ever tried to be someone you're not? Why is it important to be yourself?
   (Accept any answers.)

FOLLOW-UP ACTIVITIES

1. FRUIT SALAD

This activity shows how people view things differently. Draw pictures of fruit on colored paper or cut them out of magazines. Have each student select a picture. Then ask the students to describe what they like about that fruit. Tell the students they are going to make fruit salad. Ask which fruit they would like to leave *out* of the salad. Allow for free discussion and listen as other students justify why that fruit should be left *in* the salad.

2. THE MIRROR BOX

Glue a mirror inside one end of a shoebox. Cut a hole in the other end of the shoebox. Tell the students what they see in the box is very special. Each student should quietly look inside the box and pass it to the next person. After all the students have looked inside the box, ask what they saw. Of course, they will all say, "Me!"

3. DIFFERENT BUT IMPORTANT

This is an excellent activity to show that we are all different, but all are important. Give the students pictures of cars from which different parts are missing. Ask them to discuss what the missing parts do and how the cars would work or be safe without them. For older students, you could use a writing assignment without including the letter "E."

4. WHAT WOULD YOU DO?

Make a copy of page 37 for each student. Tell the students to follow the directions and share their story endings with the group.

5. BEN "BRAINS" BROCCOLI WORD SEARCH

Make a copy of page 38 for each student in the group. Have them find the hidden words.

WHAT WOULD YOU DO?

Circle all the pictures that show things that you would try if others were calling you names. Mark an ✗ on the pictures of things that you would *not* try.

BEN "BRAINS" BROCCOLI WORD SEARCH

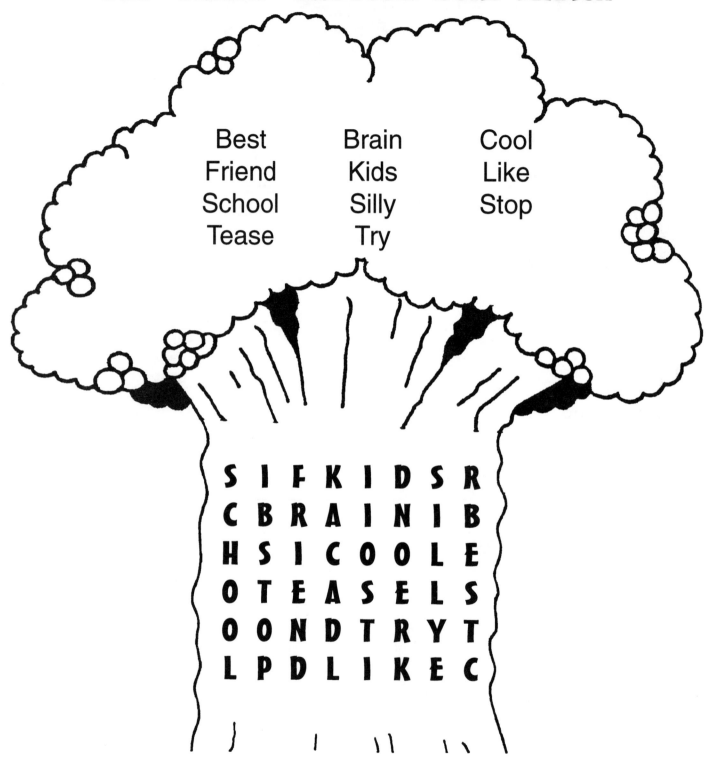

Best   Brain   Cool
Friend   Kids   Like
School   Silly   Stop
Tease   Try

S I F K I D S R
C B R A I N I B
H S I C O O L E
O T E A S E L S
O O N D T R Y T
L P D L I K E C

Find all the words listed above and circle them.
When finished, you should have circled 11 words.

38

THE GARDEN FRIENDS

Fighting

"What's going on?" asked Sweet Potato.

"It's Lucy and Sally. They're fighting!" replied Timid Tim.

Sweet Potato told everyone who was watching the argument to go and play somewhere else. Then he turned to Lucy and Sally and said, "We need to talk. But first, let's sit under the shade tree and cool off."

Sweet Potato was concerned. "Please tell me, what made you two friends start fighting?" he asked.

"Well—see—Sally Strawberry walked by me and she just reached out like this and pushed me. On purpose, too!" Lucy Lettuce said.

"No way!" exclaimed Sally Strawberry. "You did it to me. I just walked by and you pushed me, Lying Lettuce."

"Well," said Lucy, "you're an old Sticky Fingers!"

"Wait a minute," interrupted Sweet Potato. "You are both too angry to talk about this now. I'd like each of you to be by yourself for awhile and think about what has happened. We'll talk later."

IDENTIFY THE PROBLEM

A little while later, Sweet Potato called the girls together and said, "Girls, I would like to start by talking about a feeling word called *anger*. Do you think it is ever OK to feel angry?"

"No," Lucy Lettuce answered quickly.

"No," agreed Sally Strawberry. "Being angry gets us in trouble!"

"Getting angry is *bad*," said Lucy Lettuce.

"Well, guess what?" asked Sweet Potato. "It really is OK to feel angry. All of us feel differently at different times. Sometimes we feel *happy*. Sometimes we feel *sad*, and sometimes we may even feel *angry* or *mad*."

"But, Sweet Potato," argued Lucy Lettuce, "it's bad to feel angry!"

"No it isn't," answered Sweet Potato. "It's OK to feel angry. Even *I* get angry sometimes. Both kids and adults get angry. But it's how you *show* your anger that matters."

"What do you mean, Sweet Potato?" asked Sally Strawberry.

"Well," answered Sweet Potato, "some people show their anger by fighting or using angry words. For example, let's think about an adult who has a job. Do you think adults ever get angry with the people they work with, maybe even with their boss?"

"Sure they do," Sally Strawberry replied. "My mom came home so mad one day and she said she would like to just slap her boss!"

"OK, that's what I mean," said Sweet Potato. "But… did she do it?"

"Of course not!" said Sally.

"So you see," said Sweet Potato, "maybe she felt like slapping her boss, but she did not *do* it. She was able to control her anger!"

"Now," continued Sweet Potato, "let's think about what might have happened if she had not controlled her anger and had slapped her boss."

"They could have both been hurt," said Sally.

"That's right," agreed Lucy, "and then the police might have arrested your mom."

"That's right," said Sweet Potato, "and what about your mom's job?"

"I bet she would have been fired," said Sally, "and that would have been terrible."

"You're right," agreed Sweet Potato. "But these things didn't happen, because Sally's mom chose to control her anger. Do you think losing control of your anger makes things better or worse?"

"Worse!" Sally and Lucy said together.

"Now, tell me what usually happens to the kids at school when they lose control of their anger and start fighting," said Sweet Potato.

"Well," answered Lucy, "they get in trouble with the teacher and they get punished. Sometimes the principal even sends them home."

"When kids start fighting, does it make it better or worse for them?" Sweet Potato asked.

"Worse!" Sally and Lucy answered together.

"But sometimes I get so mad, I feel like I could explode! I have to do *something*!" Sally said in an excited voice.

"Yes," Sweet Potato answered, "you *do* have to get that anger out. But you have a choice! You may choose how to get it out."

"What do you mean?" asked Lucy.

Sweet Potato answered, "I mean that sometimes when someone is bothering you, you may choose to ignore that person. Just look the other way and pretend no one is there. Usually, the teaser will leave you alone if you don't pay any attention, and whenever you feel angry, try closing your eyes and slowly counting to 10."

"Why would I do that?" asked Sally.

"Because," continued Sweet Potato, "as you are slowly counting, you will have time to calm down and let your anger 'cool off.' "

"Well, I guess that does make sense, but I think it would be hard to just walk away sometimes," said Sally.

"You're right. At first it will be hard," agreed Sweet Potato. "Controlling your anger will take a lot of practice. Why don't we think about it, and then make a list of different things that you might do instead of fighting or saying angry words, whenever you feel angry."

LIST YOUR ALTERNATIVES

Sally answered first, "If somebody is bothering me, I can tell a parent, a teacher, or another adult."

Then Lucy said, "We could ignore that person."

"Or we could just close our eyes and count to 10," Sally reminded Lucy.

**10-9-8-7-6
5-4-3-2-1**

"Hey, we could even start at 10 and count backwards!" giggled Lucy.

"I feel like hitting someone whenever I get angry," said Sally. "But maybe I could just hit a punching bag or a pillow!"

Lucy laughed, "If you did that, you wouldn't get in trouble for fighting."

Sweet Potato looked pleased when he said, "Girls, you have some very good ideas. Just be sure to remember that fighting with your fists or with angry words doesn't solve problems. It only makes things worse. Let's look at your list now. Decide which one of your ideas you might try the next time you feel angry. I'm sure that if you put your heads together and really try, you will be able to think of many other ways to control your anger."

CHOOSE AN ALTERNATIVE

"I wonder which ideas Lucy and Sally will choose?" Sweet Potato asked himself. What would *you* do?

IMPLEMENT YOUR CHOICE

QUESTIONS FOR DISCUSSION

1. List two negative ways that Lucy and Sally showed their anger at the beginning of the story.
   (Fighting with their fists and using angry words.)

2. We all know that fighting can hurt. Can angry words hurt, too? How? Name some words that hurt.
   (Yes. Have the students name some ways words hurt people. Write the students' ideas on the chalkboard or on a large piece of paper. Have the students name some words that hurt people and write those words down, too.)

3. What are some negative things that may happen if you lose control of your anger?
   (Accept any appropriate answers.)

4. Do you know any adults or kids who have lost control of their anger? What did they do? How did that make you feel?
   (Emphasize that names should not be mentioned. Accept any appropriate answers.)

5. Have *you* ever lost control of your anger? What did you do? How did that make you feel?
   (Accept any answer.)

6. Name some ways that you can get rid of your anger without fighting.
   (Punch a pillow, take a walk, read a book, get away from the situation, etc.)

FOLLOW-UP ACTIVITIES

1. ANGER ALTERNATIVES

The following alternatives can be used to distract a disruptive student: tearing newspaper or magazines saved for that purpose, pounding clay or a pillow, squeezing a ball, fingerpainting, running on the playground, and writing down or drawing a picture of what is causing the anger, then tearing up the picture and throwing away your anger.

2. COOL-DOWN EXERCISES

Teach these exercises to the students so they will know how to relax in tense situations: slow, deep breaths; neck rolls; stretching; slowly counting to 10.

3. WHAT WOULD YOU DO?

Reproduce a copy of page 51 for each student in the group. Have the students follow the directions, complete, and color the page.

4. ANGER THERMOMETER

Draw a thermometer on a large sheet of paper. Insert a wide red ribbon to show the rise or fall in temperature. Mark the anger points on the thermometer: 1-not angry, 2-a little angry, 3-angry, 4-very angry, 5-out-of-control. Discuss several anger-provoking situations with the class, and use the thermometer to show how each situation makes you feel. Reproduce a copy of page 52 for each student in the group. Tell the students to complete the page. Then, discuss their answers and the various anger alternatives.

5. "KEEP YOUR COOL" CONTRACT

The *Keep Your Cool Contract* may be used with individuals who are having difficulty controlling their anger. Reproduce a copy of page 53 for the student and any significant others (counselor, teacher, parent, etc.) in the student's life.

6. "KEEP YOUR COOL" CERTIFICATE

Reproduce a copy of page 54 for students who demonstrate the ability to "keep their cool" in anger-provoking situations.

WHAT WOULD YOU DO?

Circle the pictures of things that you might want to try the next time you get angry.

ANGER THERMOMETERS

Use a crayon to chart how high your temperature would rise in each of the given situations.

I got a bad
grade on a test.

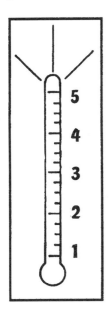

My little brother tore
up my homework.

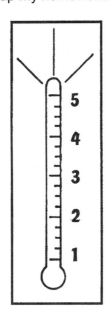

Someone teased me
and called me a name.

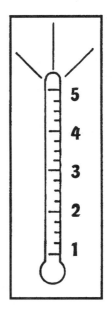

Someone pushed in
front of me in line.

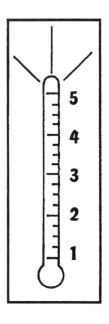

I have to be
last in line.

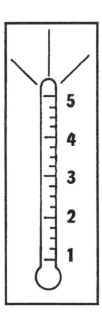

My friend wants to play
with someone else.

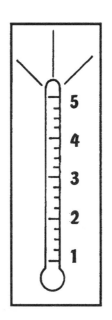

The teacher makes me
stay in during recess.

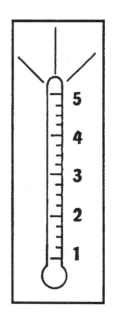

The teacher doesn't
call on me.

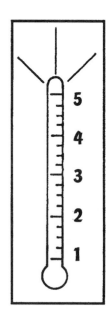

KEEP YOUR COOL CONTRACT

I, _____, agree to "keep my cool" whenever I get angry at school. I will control my anger in the following ways:

1. _____

2. _____

3. _____

If I am able to "keep my cool" for a period of ____ (weeks/ days), I will be rewarded with _____ .
(SOMETHING "COOL")

Date beginning: _____ Date ending: _____

_____
(STUDENT'S SIGNATURE)

KEEP YOUR COOL
Certificate

Presented to

_____

For
Keeping Your Cool
and
Controlling Your Anger

LUCY LETTUCE

Lying

The story begins in the *Good Neighbor Garden.* Lucy is crying. Lucy's conscience, Lindy Ladybug, is talking to her.

"I tried to warn you about lying, Lucy," whispered Lindy Ladybug.

"Lucy! What has you so upset?" asked Sweet Potato.

"Oh, Sweet Potato," cried Lucy, "my mom is mad at me, my teacher is mad at me, my friends are mad at me…"

"Wait a minute!" Sweet Potato interrupted. "I'm your friend, and I'm not mad at you. I'd like to listen if you feel like talking about it."

Lucy was kind of scared to tell Sweet Potato what had happened. She was afraid that if Sweet Potato knew the story, he would be mad at her, too. But she felt so awful about keeping the truth inside that she decided to take a chance and tell Sweet Potato the truth.

"It all started one night at home," began Lucy. "I was in the kitchen, talking to my mother, when…"

57

"Lucy, finish your homework so we can go to the ball game," said Mom.

"I've *already* finished it!" replied Lucy.

"Lucy, you know you haven't even *started* your homework," warned Lindy Ladybug.

"It's OK, Lindy," answered Lucy. " I'll get up early in the morning and do my homework. Mom will never know the difference."

"Oh no, this will never work," Lindy Ladybug sighed.

The next morning, Lucy's mother woke her and told her to get up and get dressed. "Lucy, Lucy, I told you to get up 30 minutes ago!" she called. "You're going to have to hurry."

Suddenly, Lucy remembered she had not done her homework. "Mom," she whined, "I don't feel very well. May I stay home today?"

"L-U-C-Y," gasped Lindy Ladybug. "What are you doing? You *know* you're not sick."

Just then, Mom came into the room with a thermometer. She put the thermometer in Lucy's mouth, waited a few minutes, then took it out. "Lucy," said Mom, "you don't have a temperature. I think you just stayed up too late last night. I think you'll be fine. You better get dressed, eat, and go out to the bus stop. Hurry now! You don't have much time."

Lucy made it to the bus stop just in time. When the bus arrived at her school, Lucy walked into her classroom. Right after Lucy sat down, Miss Asparagus said, "Class, please pass your homework to the front of the room."

When Charlie passed his paper to Lucy, she erased his name and wrote *her* name in its place.

Miss Asparagus looked at the homework papers, then asked, "Joyce, Sally, Jake, where are your papers?" Then she said, "Charlie, I don't see your paper, either, and this is the second day you didn't turn in any homework. You will have to stay in during recess."

"But Miss Asparagus—I *did* turn it in. Lucy, you saw me," protested Charlie. "I passed it up to you, Lucy. Don't you remember?"

"I'm sorry, Charlie. I didn't see your paper," answered Lucy.

"There you go again, Lucy!" reminded Lindy Ladybug.

During recess, Lucy sat in a swing, dragging her feet in the dust. Lindy Ladybug sat on Lucy's shoulder. "You know, Lucy, you would feel a lot better if you told Miss Asparagus the truth about your homework," said Lindy. "It's not fair for Charlie to have to stay in during recess."

"I know it's not fair, but he's already missed his recess," Lucy said. "How can it help if I tell the truth now? I just won't tell any more lies," she promised.

When recess was over, Miss Asparagus called Lucy to her desk. She said, "Lucy, I've been comparing today's homework with some of your other papers. The hand-writing doesn't look the same. In fact, what you turned in today looks like *Charlie's* handwriting. Can you explain why?"

Lindy Ladybug jumped up and down on Lucy's shoulder. "Here's you chance!" Lindy said excitedly. "Tell the truth!"

Lucy pretended not to hear Lindy. "Miss Asparagus," she answered quickly. "I was in a hurry! That's why my handwriting looks different."

Miss Asparagus was sure Lucy was not telling the truth, so she said, "I think I'll give your mother a call."

"That's what happened, Sweet Potato," said Lucy. "I didn't mean to tell lies. And I sure didn't want Charlie to get in trouble."

"What's your mother going to think when she gets that call from Miss Asparagus?" asked Sweet Potato.

"I'm afraid to think about what she's going to say," Lucy cried. "I was just going to tell one little lie. Then everything would be OK. But that's not the way it happened. Nothing is OK now!"

IDENTIFY THE PROBLEM

"Lucy, what do you think you could do to make things better?" asked Sweet Potato.

Lindy Ladybug couldn't stand it any longer. "Tell everyone the truth, Lucy," she begged.

"Well," Lucy said, "even though I know I'm going to get punished, I'm going to tell Mom the truth. I think I'd better tell Miss Asparagus what I did and also tell Charlie that I'm sorry."

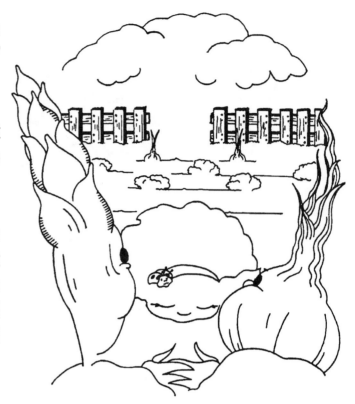

#1
#2
#3
#4

"It sounds like you're on the right track now," answered Sweet Potato. "But what about next time? What are you going to do then?"

LIST THE ALTERNATIVES

64

"Next time?" Lucy asked loudly. "There won't *be* a next time. I won't tell even the *first* lie. I won't tell it even if it means I can't have my way or I get in trouble."

"That sounds great," Sweet Potato said. "But what if you forget?"

Lucy thought about that for a few minutes. Then she said, "Well… I guess I could say the dog ate my homework. No one else would get into trouble if I did that. So that would be only a little lie."

"Or if I do tell a lie, I could say I'm sorry and then tell the truth. I could try to make up for it," Lucy added.

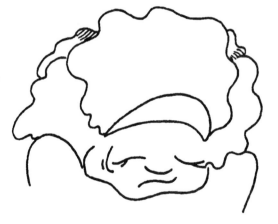

"Maybe I should just keep my mouth shut and never talk again," Lucy said.

"It sounds like you have a lot to think about," said Sweet Potato. "I think you realize now that no one benefits from telling a lie. Let's look at the different things you could do instead of telling a lie. Let's see which idea might really help you the next time you are tempted to lie."

CHOOSE AN ALTERNATIVE

"I wonder which choice Lucy will make," thought Sweet Potato. What would *you* choose?

IMPLEMENT YOUR CHOICE

QUESTIONS FOR DISCUSSION

1. What is a *lie*?
   (Accept and discuss the students' answers. Guide the discussion so that the conclusion will be that a lie is any statement that is not true.)

2. What was Lucy's first lie?
   (She told her mother she had finished her homework even though she had not.)

3. Did Lucy stop with one lie or did her first lie lead to more?
   (After Lucy told the first lie, she had to keep telling more lies so she would not be caught in the first lie.)

4 Is it ever OK to tell a lie?
   (Talk about things like telling a stranger who calls on the telephone that your mother is home when she's not and why it is OK to tell a lie like that. Talk about other times when it is OK to lie. Then talk about times when it is not OK to lie.)

5. Have *you* ever told a lie?
   (Students should raise their hands to respond to this question. The leader should also raise his/her hand to show that almost everyone has told a lie at one time or another. Talk about how it feels when you lie.)

6. What is a *conscience*?
   (Refer to Lindy Ladybug in the story. Emphasize to the group that a conscience is not something you see as Lucy Lettuce saw Lindy, but something you feel that reminds you what you are doing is either right or wrong.)

7. Has *your* conscience ever talked to *you*? Did you listen?
   (Accept any answers.)

8. What unpleasant things can happen when you tell a lie?
   (You may want to list the students' answers on the chalkboard or on a large piece of paper.)

FOLLOW-UP ACTIVITIES

1. SITUATION CARDS

From old magazines or workbooks, cut out pictures depicting childhood "accidents" such as spilled milk, broken dishes, dirty clothes, etc. Paste the pictures on index cards. Have each student pick a card and explain what he/she would say and do if this accident happened to him/her.

2. WE CANNOT TELL A LIE

Read the students the story of George Washington and the cherry tree. Have them draw a picture about a time when they told the truth when it would have been easier to lie. Display the students' pictures on a bulletin board labeled "We Cannot Tell a Lie."

3. PINOCCHIO

Read the story of Pinocchio or show a filmstrip/video of the tale. Ask the students to identify Pinocchio's conscience and explain how it helped him tell the truth when he wanted to lie.

4. MY CONSCIENCE

Have the students think of a symbol to represent their conscience and then draw a picture showing how it has helped or could help them.

5. WHAT WOULD YOU DO?

Reproduce a copy of page 69 for each student in the group. Tell the students to follow the directions on the page and complete the activity. When the students have completed the activity, they may share their decisions and story endings with the group.

6. LADYBUG

Reproduce a copy of page 70 for each student in the group. Tell the students to follow the directions on the page and complete the activity. When the students have completed the activity, have them share what they wrote with the group.

WHAT WOULD YOU DO?

Circle the choices you might pick if you were tempted to tell a lie. Mark an **✗** on the pictures of things you would not do.

| Don't tell the first lie. | Say the dog did it. |
| Say, "I'm sorry." | Never talk again. |

Draw a picture of how the story of Lucy Lettuce might end.

LADYBUG

In this story, Lucy's conscience was Lindy Ladybug. Lindy tried to help Lucy do the right thing. Has *your* conscience ever talked to *you*? Inside the Ladybug, write down some things your conscience has said to you.

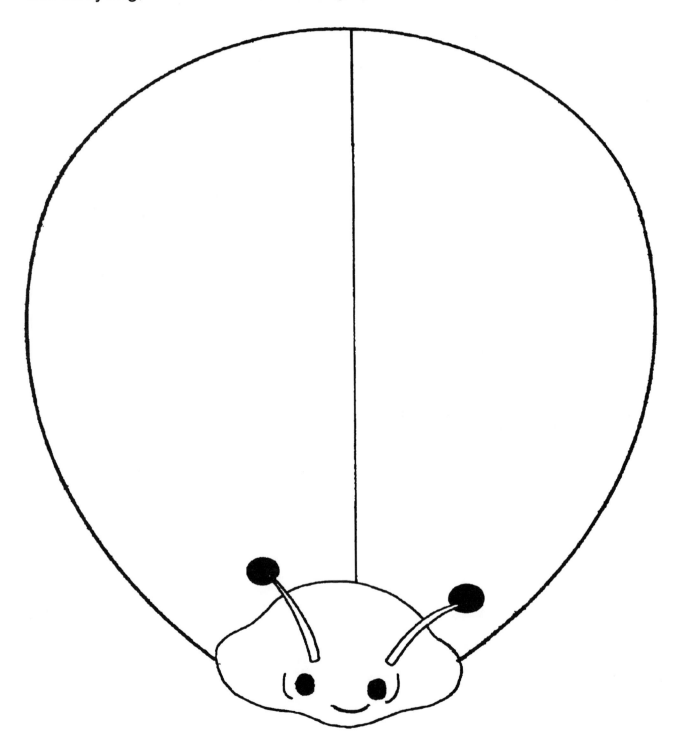

SALLY STRAWBERRY

Stealing

"Hello! My name is Sweet Potato.
I live here, in the *Good Neighbor Garden.*
Come with me, and I'll show you around the garden."

Tim Tomato was crying when Sweet Potato entered the garden.

"What's going on?" asked Sweet Potato.

"It's Sally!" answered Tim. "She's always taking our things!"

"She steals everything when we're not looking!" added Lucy Lettuce.

"Now she's taken my hat!" Carl Carrot said angrily.

73

"Oh! You can have your old hat back. It's ugly anyway!" yelled Sally Strawberry, as she threw the hat to Carl.

IDENTIFY THE PROBLEM

"Sally, I'd like for you to take a walk with me," said Sweet Potato.

"Sure, Sweet Potato," she answered, "I don't want to hang around here."

74

"Sally, let's talk about what just happened," Sweet Potato suggested. "This isn't the first time something like this has happened. Do you remember that last week you took Ben Broccoli's book when he wasn't looking?"

"Yes, I remember," answered Sally.

"What makes you take things that don't belong to you?" asked Sweet Potato.

"I don't know!" cried Sally. "I just wanted it!"

"Do you think it's fair to take things that don't belong to you?" asked Sweet Potato.

"I don't know," Sally replied angrily. "But I know I don't want to talk about it anymore!"

"All right," Sweet Potato said, "we don't have to talk about it."

Sweet Potato knew he should find something else to talk about so he said, "By the way, Sally, I like the bow in your hair. It is very pretty."

"Thank you!" Sally smiled. "It's my favorite bow. That's why I wear it all the time!"

Sweet Potato noticed it was beginning to get dark so he said, "Well, it's getting late. You'd better go home now, Sally. Give me a hug before you leave."

Sally gave Sweet Potato a big hug and ran down the path calling, "Good-bye, Sweet Potato." She was in such a hurry to get home that she did not notice her bow had fallen off her head and onto the ground.

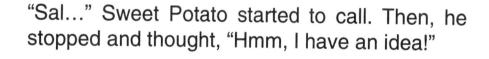

"Sal..." Sweet Potato started to call. Then, he stopped and thought, "Hmm, I have an idea!"

As Sally ran home, she put her hand on her head. She felt all around, but her bow was not there. She got very upset and cried, "My bow! My pretty bow! Where is my B-O-W?"

Sally turned around and started to go back to look for her bow when she saw Sweet Potato carrying it. "Why Sweet Potato!" she cried. "You took my bow! Give it back! It doesn't belong to you. It's *my* bow! You're my friend. I trusted you!"

"Come here, Sally," said Sweet Potato. "Yes, it is your bow, but I didn't take it. As you were leaving, it fell to the ground. Let's talk about how you felt when you thought I had stolen it."

"Awful, just awful!" cried Sally. "It made me feel all funny inside."

"So, how do you think your friends felt when you took their things?" asked Sweet Potato.

"I guess they felt pretty awful," Sally said sadly.

78

"You're probably right," agreed Sweet Potato. "I'm sure they felt the same way you do now. Sally, ask yourself this question and think about it: Should I take things that don't belong to me?"

"No," answered Sally. "I'm sorry, Sweet Potato. I shouldn't have taken those things."

"Now, I think you understand how your friends felt," said Sweet Potato. "Let's think about what you might do the next time you are tempted to take things that don't belong to you."

LIST YOUR ALTERNATIVES

"Well…" began Sally. "I could remember how upset I felt to think something had been stolen from me. That might keep me from doing it to someone else."

"I guess if I asked nicely, maybe my friends would let me borrow their things for awhile. I could say something like, 'Please may I borrow your book? I'd like to read it.' "

"If I *do* steal something, I could take it back and say, 'I'm, sorry. I'm really sorry. I won't do it again!' "

"Or I could try to earn some money to buy the things I want."

"Your ideas are very good, Sally," said Sweet Potato. " Now go back and look at each of your choices and decide which one you will try the next time you feel like taking something that doesn't belong to you. Remember, if one idea doesn't work—DON'T GIVE UP! You may try something else or we can talk about it again."

CHOOSE AN ALTERNATIVE

#1
#2
#3
#4

I wonder which idea Sally will try. What choice would you make?

IMPLEMENT YOUR CHOICE

QUESTIONS FOR DISCUSSION

1. Why were the children calling Sally "Sticky Fingers?"
   (Explain that the term "sticky fingers" is a name used to describe people who steal things. It means that someone else's belongings are stuck to the fingers of the thief. The children called Sally this name because she took their things.)

2. Is it ever OK to take something that is not yours?
   (Accept any answer. However, be sure to have the students explain the reasoning behind their answers. If there is a questionable answer have the students discuss it as a group and reach a common agreement.)

3. What did Sally think Sweet Potato had done with her bow?
   (Sally thought Sweet Potato had stolen her bow.)

4. How did Sally feel when she thought one of her friends had taken something that belonged to her?
   (She felt awful.)

5. Have you ever taken anything that did not belong to you?
   How did it make you feel?
   (Accept any answer.)

6. What are some things you could do if you are tempted to steal?
   (You may want to list the students' answers on the chalkboard or on a large piece of paper.)

FOLLOW-UP ACTIVITIES

1. "WHAT IF" GAME

Ask the children: "What If" Sally had decided it was OK to take something since her friend had something else just like it and wouldn't miss it anyway? Discuss other "What If" situations.

2. SELF-ESTEEM ACTIVITIES

Discussions about stealing often lead to negative feelings of self. Therefore, self-esteem activities are important.

   a. Children may look through magazines and cut out pictures of things that make them feel good. They may share their favorite picture with the group.

   b. "I'm Thumbody Special." Using an ink pad, make a print of each child's thumb. Show the children how to make a thumb print critter by using markers or crayons. Display the thumb critters on a bulletin board.

3. SKIT

Have the students develop a skit using some of the alternatives mentioned in the story.

4. FEELINGS DISCUSSION

Discuss different feelings (disappointment, anger, pride). After the discussion, have the students describe how these feelings apply to different parts of the story.

5. WHAT WOULD YOU DO?

Reproduce a copy of page 84 for each student in the group. Have the students follow the directions, complete, and color the page.

6. MATCHING

Reproduce a copy of page 85 for each student in the group. Have them follow the directions. Discuss the feelings the different faces represent.

7. SALLY STRAWBERRY'S MAZE

Reproduce a copy of page 86 for each student in the group. Have the students find their way through the maze. When the students have completed the maze, discuss how alternatives relate to problem-solving.

WHAT WOULD YOU DO?

Circle the pictures of things you might try if you were tempted to steal. Mark an ✗ on the pictures of things you would not want to try.

I could remember how it felt when something had been stolen from me.

I could ask my friends to let me borrow their things for awhile.

If I stole something, I could take it back and say, "I'm sorry."

I could try to earn some money to buy the things I want.

MATCHING

Draw a line from the faces to the feeling words that match each expression.

ANGRY

HAPPY

SAD

EMBARRASSED

SALLY STRAWBERRY'S MAZE

Sally would like to return Carl Carrot's hat, but she doesn't know where he is in the Strawberry Patch. Help Sally find Carl Carrot. There are different paths to choose. If one path doesn't lead to Carl, take another path. Remember, there are usually at least two solutions to any problem.

TIMID TIM

Shyness

"Hello! I'm Sweet Potato. Welcome to my home in the *Good Neighbor Garden*."

"I would like you to meet my good friend, Tim Tomato."

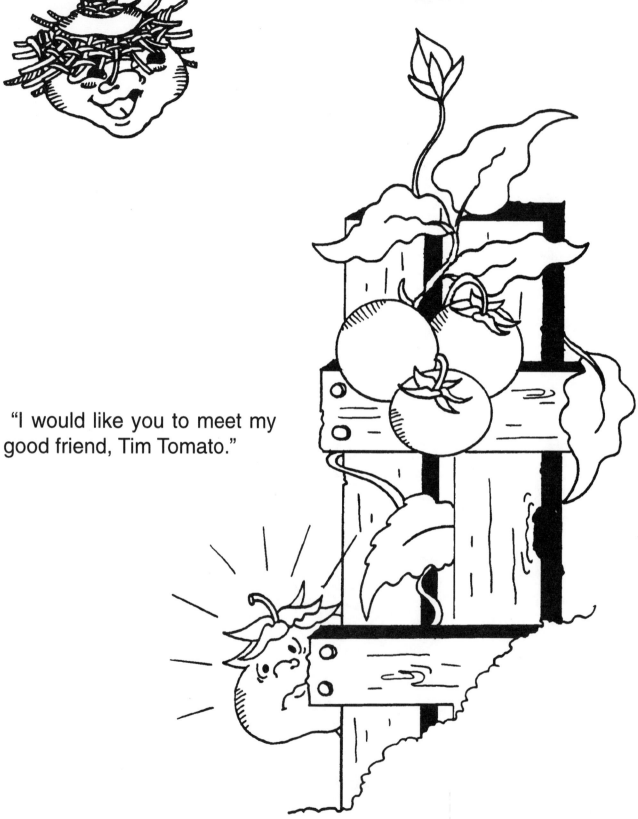

"Poor Tim," said Sweet Potato. "He is timid, or you might say shy, and sometimes his friends in the garden tease him. They call him *Timid Tim*, and that makes him sad."

"It's all right to be timid sometimes," Sweet Potato continued, "unless it makes you sad. And right now, Tim looks pretty sad."

Sweet Potato thought to himself, "I wonder how Tim might act if he only knew how special he really is. Being timid can be a problem, and I would like to help Tim feel better about himself. I'm going to see what I can do."

IDENTIFY THE PROBLEM

"First of all Tim," Sweet Potato began, "you should know how very special you are. There's no one else in this garden, or even in the whole wide world, just like you."

"Really?" Tim asked in surprise. "How can that be? There are a lot of other tomatoes in the garden!"

"Yes, of course there are," Sweet Potato agreed. "But *you* are different. That's what makes you special. Why, just look at your reflection in the pond! I think you have the nicest smile and the prettiest smooth skin of any tomato I've ever seen."

Tim looked at himself in the pond. "Do you really think so?" he asked. "Maybe I *am* special!"

"Tim, you *are* special," Sweet Potato assured him, "and you don't have to cry or hide your face when you are around others. Can you think of some things you can do when you are with your friends or meet someone new? Would you like me to help you make a list?"

Tim was not sure what Sweet Potato meant, but he was too shy to ask. So he said, "Well, OK."

LIST YOUR ALTERNATIVES

Tim thought and thought about what he could do. Finally, he said, "I could run away! That's what I feel like doing most of the time."

"Or I could just stay home by myself. Then I wouldn't ever have to worry about how I feel or how others feel about me."

A moment later, Tim looked up at Sweet Potato and said, "I could stay around *you*, Sweet Potato, because you make me feel special."

Tim kept thinking about what he could do to solve his problem. Then he remembered what Sweet Potato had told him about his smile. "I guess I could try smiling at others," Tim said. "After all, you did say I have a nice smile."

Tim thought that if he could smile, he might also be able to talk. He said, "I guess I could even say something nice to others. I know how good it makes me feel when you say nice things to me."

Hi! Would you like to play?
My name is Tim.
What's your name?

Sweet Potato was very proud of Tim's ideas. He said, "Tim, I like your ideas. Think about each idea and decide which one you like best. Try to do that the next time you are around your friends or meet someone new."

"If you try one idea and it doesn't work—DON'T GIVE UP!" Sweet Potato reminded Tim. "Look at your list again and try another idea."

CHOOSE AN ALTERNATIVE

As Sweet Potato walked away, he wondered which idea Tim Tomato would try. What choice would you make?

IMPLEMENT YOUR CHOICE

QUESTIONS FOR DISCUSSION

1. What was Tim Tomato's problem at the beginning of the story?
   (Tim was sad because his friends were teasing him.)

2. What does *timid* or *shy* mean?
   (A timid or shy person has a hard time speaking up in groups or in new situations. Shy people get embarrassed easily and do not usually like to be noticed.)

3. Have you ever been timid? How did it make you feel?
   (Accept any answer.)

4. What might you do if you are feeling a little timid?
   (Have the students answer and write their ideas on the chalkboard or on a large sheet of paper. Some ideas might be to practice talking to other people by looking in the mirror and talking, talking to a puppet, talking into a tape recorder, writing down what you want to say and reading it aloud to yourself before saying it in a group, or making a contract with yourself to make an effort to speak up in a group each week.)

5. Everyone is special in his/her own way. Describe some things that are special about you.
   (Accept any answer.)

6. Name some ways friends can be different from one another.
   (Write the students' answers on the chalkboard or on a large sheet of paper. Discuss the fact that a different race, age, religion, or interests does not prevent friendships from developing.)

FOLLOW-UP ACTIVITIES

1. PUPPETRY

Use the puppets to discuss the problem of shyness. Have one puppet suffer from the negative results of being timid. As he shivers in your arms with his head turned away from the group, explain that he is timid. Remind the students what the word *timid* means. Ask the students why they think the puppet is timid and how they can help the puppet overcome his shyness.

2. MAKING PUPPETS

Have each student design a hand puppet using a sack or sock. Using a hand puppet will help students feel less threatened when speaking in front of the group. If the other students laugh at a response, they will be laughing at the puppet, not at the student. Divide the children into pairs and use the puppets to act out the story of Timid Tim.

3. LOTTO OR BINGO

Use a Lotto or Bingo game to elicit verbal responses from the students. Students may cover their answers after they have used a complete sentence to announce that they have the number called. Example: "I have the number 15."

4. SHOW AND TELL

Arrange a special "Show-and-Tell" day for timid students. Try to find out what their particular interests are.

5. WHAT WOULD YOU DO?

Reproduce a copy of page 100 for each student in the group. Tell the students to follow the directions on the page and share their decisions with the group.

6. COMPLETE TIM

Reproduce a copy of page 101 for each student in the group and tell them to complete the picture of Timid Tim. Display their pictures on a bulletin board.

7. TIM TOMATO MATCHING

Reproduce a copy of page 102 for each student in the group and tell the students to match the faces. Discuss the feelings the faces represent.

WHAT WOULD YOU DO?

Circle the pictures of things you might want to try when you feel timid. Mark an **X** on the pictures of things you would not want to try.

Draw a picture of how you think the story of Timid Tim might end.

COMPLETE TIM

Tim Tomato is **Happy**. Draw a **Smile** on his face. Color Tim Tomato **Red**.

TIM TOMATO MATCHING

Draw a line connecting
the faces that look like each other.

My name is_____

FINGER PUPPET PROGRAMS AVAILABLE FROM MAR*CO

FROGGY & FRIENDS II
Kathie Guild

The ever-popular Froggy & Friends Series is now available in a second edition. Published in one book, Froggy's adventures include: tattling, bullying, doing your best, name calling, prejudice, and bragging. Each topic includes an illustrated story, discussion questions, and multiple reproducible activities. Topics can be completed in one or more than one session. Also included are six new finger puppets (frog, bear, rabbit, skunk, snake, and wolf) that can be used to enhance the presentation. For use with individuals, small groups, or classrooms. **Grade levels: K–3.**
FF968 • $32.95/6 STORIES & 6 FINGER PUPPETS

FROGGY & FRIENDS I
Kathie Guild

Froggy teaches social skills. This exciting program combines stories, finger puppets, and numerous activities to help students learn to make and keep friends, use good manners, develop self-esteem, listen carefully, deal with peer pressure, follow school safety rules, return things that are found, and learn good lunchroom behavior. Included are eight stories and nine finger puppets (frog, bee, raccoon, pig, bird, kangaroo, octopus, worm, and mouse). Each program can be used separately or all can be used in a sequential presentation. For use with individuals, small groups, or classrooms. **Grade levels: K–3.**
FF925 • $32.95/8 STORIES & 9 FINGER PUPPETS

FEARS AWAY SERIES
Arden Martenz

Everyone must learn to deal with internal conflicts, and fears are a source of internal conflict. This program teaches students to resolve the conflicts they have with themselves over their fears of being bullied or teased, academic mistakes, embarrassment, scary movies, natural disasters, and the dark. Each topic is presented in a story format, has related discussion questions and reproducible activities, and uses finger puppets. Includes six books and five finger puppets (buffalo, owl, mountain goat, prairie dog, and coyote). For use with individuals, small groups, or classrooms. **Grade levels: 2–5.**
FA941 • $32.95/6 BOOKS & 5 FINGER PUPPETS

TO ORDER, CALL: 1-800-448-2197